Picture Oregon

Picture Oregon

PORTRAITS OF
THE UNIVERSITY
OF OREGON

UNIVERSITY OF OREGON · EUGENE · 1994

Copyright 1994 University of Oregon Books
Eugene OR 97403-1282

ISBN 0-87114-287-2

Principal photographer: Jack Liu

Contributing photographers:

Christine Beltran (PAGE 106)
George Beltran (PAGES 4, 13, 23, 38, 48, 49, 51, 107, DUST JACKET BACK)
John Giustina (PAGES 30, 31)
Roseanne Olson (PAGE 6)
Oscar Palmquist (PAGES 1, 39, 44)
Jim Sundberg (PAGE 110)

Historical photographs: Courtesy of K. Keith Richard, University Archivist,
University Archives, University of Oregon

Contributors, University of Oregon:

Text: James McChesney
Editors: Adel Brown, Barbara Edwards
Title: Frances Milligan
Designer: George Beltran

Producers, University of Oregon:

Brodie Remington, Vice President, Public Affairs and Development
Matthew Dyste, Director, Office of Merchandising

Color: Spectrum West, Inc., Beaverton, Oregon

Printer: Schultz/Wack/Weir, Portland, Oregon

Binders: Lincoln & Allen Bindery, Portland

Clockwise from top center:
Ellen Condon McCornack
Robert S. Bean
M. S. Wallis
John Wesley Johnson
George Washburn
Charles Whiteaker

Dedicated to the members of the Class of 1878, the university's first graduating class, Ellen Condon McCornack, Robert S. Bean, M. S. Wallis, George Washburn, and Charles Whiteaker, and to the university's first president, John Wesley Johnson.

Introduction

BY DAVE FROHNMAYER
President, University of Oregon

SOMETHING remarkable happens when friends take a leisurely walk together. Conversation becomes easy and relaxed, a sense of familiarity and confidence grows, and details of the surroundings, perhaps previously unnoticed, become personal—even sentimental.

For young women and men attending the University of Oregon a century ago, walking and conversing together was a social art celebrated at the Walk Around, where, under bright lights and in time to lively music, students walked together up and down the aisles in Villard Hall. Undoubtedly, romances and lifelong friendships unfolded as students made polite conversation while strolling arm in arm at this once-a-year occasion.

It is in the spirit of the Walk Around—friends getting acquainted or reacquainted, conversations agreeable, surroundings comfortable—that *Picture*

Oregon is offered. We invite you to walk through the University of Oregon campus, to wander along with us as we point out architectural details on historic buildings and reminisce about the people and events that influenced more than 100 years of history at the University of Oregon.

We will show you façades and fish ponds, archways and artwork, intricacies of glass, wood, and stone while telling you about university builders, leaders, students, and student life from the school's earliest days.

Like warm words between friends, the photographs and anecdotes within these pages are expressions of a larger whole—highlights of a rich history, glimpses of distinct architecture, a pleasant diversion.

So step again on the worn stone stair of the Knight Library as, together, we picture Oregon.

I
Promise and Hope

*L*OOKING UP from the valley on a clear spring morning, they saw majestic snowy peaks shouldering through that ragged gap in the Cascades, north-facing hills eroded by the ages, a western mountain range that turned to shadows at sunset—a landscape of promise and hope.

Pioneers of the Oregon Trail came here, to the West, for reasons as varied as the individuals themselves. They came to a frontier and built a community with the memories of what they had left behind and with the dreams of what they had traveled so far to find.

Oregon. Namesake and endpoint of the Oregon Trail. A 96,000-square-mile symbol of a proud and growing nation. Part of that pride—and the ideals it engendered—was the demand for a place to educate its people.

State lawmakers, even in the 1800s, were forced to measure ideals against resources. Yet in 1872, they passed a bill that granted authority to establish the state university in Eugene.

There are stories that pioneer, civic leader, and publisher Harrison R. Kincaid was responsible for bringing the University of Oregon to Eugene. The 1872 legislative session was coming to a close, and

when Kincaid realized that the university bill was near the bottom of a thick stack of legislation yet to be considered, he took matters into his own hands. His story—perhaps true, perhaps improved upon—was documented years later in the Portland *Oregonian*:

    "Slipping unnoticed into the deserted room where the package of bills was kept, the resourceful pioneer and hometown patriot stealthily untied the binding ribbon and slid the university bill off of the bottom and placed it on top of the pile. (Or so he eventually confided to his family.) This action, Kincaid said later, is what saved the University of Oregon for Eugene."

    While sleight of hand by one man may have given official authority for the University of Oregon to locate in Eugene, it was the hard work by many others that enabled the completion of the first building, Deady Hall, on a rise overlooking the Willamette River. The building was to be financed through a $30,000 bond issue and $20,000 in private donations. But there was trouble. The effects of a financial panic in 1871 lingered, and the bond issue was rescinded by the courts.

    Money was scarce, but dedication and commitment were abundant. The legislature granted an extension. Benjamin Dorris, a Eugene-area attorney, donated tin to cover a partly completed building. Newspapers outlined the advantages of a university in Eugene, and local supporters canvassed the countryside for cows, chickens, pigs,

crops—anything that could be converted to funds for the building. Dances, socials, and concerts raised capital, and a children's crusade for pennies, nickels, and dimes yielded $1,750.

Construction continued, and on October 16, 1876, the doors of Deady Hall opened.

Lacking the formal background for entry to Yale, Johnson was admitted as a special student and, four years later, was graduated sixth in his class. He taught. He worked in mines. He overcame health problems. And in 1876, he was selected by the board of regents to be the first president of the University of Oregon.

While land and a building provided a setting, it was—and is—people of vision who transformed this site into the University of Oregon.

One such person was John Wesley Johnson. Bright but unschooled, Johnson did not learn the alphabet until he was ten. After taking classes at Pacific University in Forest Grove, he and a cousin set out for Yale in New Haven, Connecticut, via San Francisco, Panama, and New York.

Other forward-looking leaders in scholarship were drawn to the university: Thomas Condon, professor of social studies and sciences; George Collier, professor of physics and chemistry; Luella Clay Carson, professor of rhetoric and dean of women; and Mary Spiller, who taught in the preparatory school that was then attached to the university.

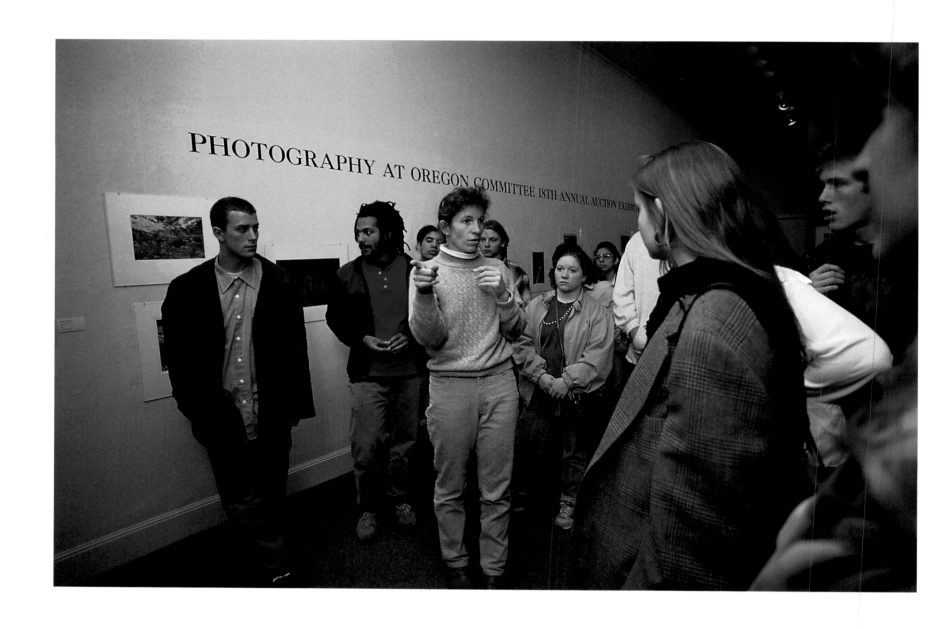

Each contributed uniquely to the vision that is the University of Oregon.

Condon was a minister who became a scientist. He combined his religious beliefs with the emerging sciences of geology, paleontology, and anthropology.

Collier came from Willamette University to teach physics and chemistry. His home became the residence of the president.

Spiller demanded the best from her students, yet she understood their needs for social events. She helped organize the literary societies that became the social focal points of the university's early days.

Carson came to the University of Oregon in 1888 to teach rhetoric, but for nearly a quarter of a century taught much more. Her areas of expertise as a teacher were oral and written composition, but outside the classroom Carson specialized in conduct and taste. Appointed dean of women in 1899, she set the rules of proper conduct for students, determining the appropriate degree of cheering by women at football games, regulating the proper distance between men and women on campus, and judging that women should not play the "rough and unladylike" game of basketball.

Strict discipline was maintained at the university, as attested to by the following entries in faculty-meeting minutes:

"April 27, 1882—President to investigate cases of student intemperance.

"September 28, 1882—Young ladies and gentlemen assigned to different classrooms and required to use different stairways.

"April 10, 1895—Young ladies forbidden to wear their gymnasium suits outside the gymnasium."

II
Walk Around

ONLY ONE social event at the university, the Walk Around, was considered proper and in good taste.

"I came to the university in 1888," wrote one female student, "as a student of the Preparatory Department. At that time, there was but one social function allowed on campus each year, and that was called the Walk Around. I tell you, it was fun. . . .

"You arrived at Villard [Hall], took off wraps in the Ladies Room, puffed up your front and back bangs and adjusted your bustle. Then you went up to the auditorium, where you found

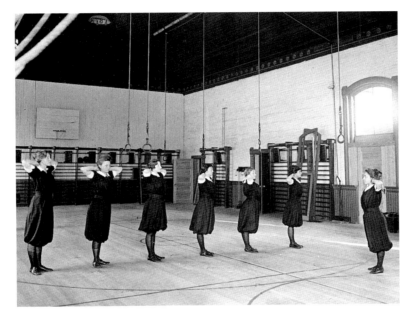

the incandescent lights very bright. . . .

"Then came a young man and said, 'May I have the pleasure of this Walk Around?'

"You stepped into the aisle, with him offering his arm, and off you went, up one aisle and down the other, round and round the middle section, keeping step with the music, which was very good. When the music stopped he took you back to your seat, and said, 'Thank you,' and returned to the other young men. . . .

"The Walk Around began at eight o'clock

and continued until ten, when the strains of Home Sweet Home hinted that the one social event of the year on campus was over, but the memories lived on!"

Maintaining good taste and discipline was not the only challenge of the time. A financial crisis struck in 1881 and promises of donations were not kept. The courts threatened closure of the university.

Northwest newspapers carried the story, and Henry Villard, a railroad promoter and friend of board of regents president Matthew Deady, immediately underwrote the university's debt. Villard followed up with an endowment of $50,000 in railroad bonds, which still produce revenue to support the library.

By the turn of the century, however, even with Villard's generous gifts, the University of Oregon was again on shaky financial ground.

Members of the faculty worked without pay, lighting was not available for the new Library Building, the girls' dormitory stood unfurnished, classrooms were crowded.

But then the tide turned—again with the vision and leadership of one person, Prince Lucien Campbell.

"The state is supporting the university for the benefit of the young men and women who are anxious to prepare themselves to accomplish the most in life," wrote Campbell. "No ambitious son or daughter of Oregon, blessed with good health

and the right determination, need despair of securing the benefits of a university training when so much in the way of opportunity is freely offered."

That was the vision.

Campbell, born in Missouri in 1861, moved with his family to Oregon at the age of six. Graduated from Christian College at eighteen, he taught there for three years before going east and enrolling at Harvard.

By the time Campbell returned to Oregon in 1886, he had earned a degree and had worked for a year as a reporter for the Kansas City *Star*. He taught Greek, Latin, English, physics, chemistry, psychology, and pedagogy at the State Normal School in Monmouth, and in 1898 became that institution's president.

Throughout the next decade Campbell traveled the state, aiding the development of public elementary schools, building friendships with University of Oregon presidents Charles Chapman and Frank Strong, and strengthening his abilities to meet the challenges of education in this growing state.

In 1902, when Strong resigned his position, Campbell was immediately asked by the university to become its president.

He agreed.

His presidency was marked by a period of growth unequaled until the 1950s. The university's budget grew from $47,500 to more than $700,000; the number of buildings increased from six to

twenty-one. Student enrollment grew from 345 to 3,200, and the faculty increased from two dozen to 142.

The School of Music was established in 1902, the School of Architecture in 1914. The School of Law moved from Portland to Eugene in 1915, and the School of Journalism was created in 1916. The university opened the nation's first School of Health and Physical Education in 1920, and the budget of the Medical School at Portland was increased to create the capacity for both research and teaching.

Campbell understood leadership and power and used it for the benefit of the university. He recruited a corps of excellent teachers and researchers. He expanded the curriculum to meet the needs of the state and the students, and he convinced the regents to tolerate a wide range of academic freedoms. Campbell protected professors who held unconventional views, believing that the test of a university was the freedom to express and explore ideas without fear of retribution. He protected faculty members with unpopular lifestyles or political views, including a homosexual and a socialist.

An idealist and optimist who was keenly interested in individuals, Campbell spoke at every student assembly at the beginning of the academic year and tried to visit at least once with each member of the senior class.

III
Pride and Spirit

CAMPBELL'S unflagging idealism was matched only by his solid determination to meet the brick-and-mortar needs of the growing university. He brought to campus Ellis F. Lawrence, who designed the nineteen university buildings constructed between 1915 and 1944.

During Campbell's tenure, student life progressed with a sense of pride and spirit as solid as the new buildings and programs of the time. An entry in the university yearbook, the *Oregana*, declared, "The Class of 1911 believes itself to be the most brilliant aggregation of mortals that ever favored the University of Oregon with four years of its precious time."

A sense of that "precious time" at the university was kept alive by traditions. Homecoming celebration. Bonfires. The painted O on Skinner Butte. The Millrace, which promised romance away from watchful eyes.

In athletics, the challenge was to find victory—or a good excuse. "The 1912 football season was characterized by remarkably inconsistent playing by the different teams of the Northwest," one report offered. "Oregon was the most consistently inconsistent team of them all. . . . However, this can be partly explained. . . ."

Explanations were not needed by track-and-field coach Bill Hayward. He had become a West Coast coaching legend. An *Oregana* tribute read: "'Bill' has been taking the highest honors for Oregon so regularly in the Northwest Conference that he might well be the inventor of track meets in the Northwest . . . having won nine championships out of eleven."

But by 1918, the issue of athletic performance was overshadowed by human loss as that "war over there" made its sure and steady way over here. Nearly 500 men from the University of Oregon enlisted in the armed forces; thirty-nine lives were lost.

Women, too, were active patriots overseas. Elizabeth Freeman Fox, dean of women, volunteered to serve with the YWCA, and the staff of the 1918 *Oregana* dedicated that year's issue to her as one who is "somewhere in France offering her life in the service of her country."

Concern about women's roles was prevalent. "There is a danger, perhaps, in losing sight of the fact that, for most women, the chosen vocation is that of housekeeper and homemaker," warned a university yearbook writer.

Many, however, looked forward to a changing world. Another student wrote, "Since the outbreak of the Great War, history has gained enormously in the estimation of cultured minds. . . . It supplies

the best means of inter-preting the present and even predicting the future."

When the war ended, many of those who returned rejected the conventions of the past and embraced their future as Americans of the jazz age.

Students expressed this new vision of them-selves in the *Oregana*:

"Youthful Spirit threw aside the brown books and copy paper with which he had been whiling away long hours, and said, 'There is something inside me that wants to dance.'

"Then softly over the wind came the rumble and the beat of hidden music; saxophones, kettle drums, zooming viols, sharp clarinet calls, horns, whistles, and the measured tinkle of many pianos.

And so down the years came the jazz orchestras, marching to a music that was to set the feet of Youth a-dance."

Cars replaced horses and buggies. Hemlines inched up-ward and ankles were visible. Men abandoned suit jackets and ties, trading them for sweaters and raccoon coats.

"It was a lovely time to be alive, to be in college," re-called Darle Seymour, Class of 1922. "We thought we had a free ride." The war to end all wars had been fought. The good life was just around the bend.

Not all embraced the pace of the modern world and the spirit of the age of jazz. "We believe the answer to the ugliness of jazz," wrote university president Arnold Bennett Hall, "is training in new standards of the appre-ciation of the artistic and the beautiful."

An *Oregana* writer expressed both the hope and the

challenge as the University of Oregon prepared to enter the 1930s: "Humanity as a whole . . . is becoming more and more intricate, hazardous, and interesting."

This statement would prove to be prophetic—real beyond anyone's imagination.

Earlier financial challenges paled in comparison to those faced by the nation—and the university—in the next rawboned decade of dust and scarcity.

"Serious disturbances in the life and activities of college students have been inevitable," wrote Karl W. Onthank, adviser to students. "Nearly all have less money. Some, to whom expenses were of no consequence a year or two ago, are now faced by the stark necessity for earning their own way."

Although student enrollment decreased by nearly a third from 1929 to 1933, many campus activities continued. The Don Cossack Russian Chorus, Roland Hayes, the Ballet Russe, Admiral Byrd, Duke Ellington, Martha Graham, and Jimmy Dorsey made appearances in Eugene. And the beautiful people of the day—Joe College and Betty Coed—continued to hold center court.

The theater brought valuable lessons as Henrik Ibsen's *Peer Gynt*, Noel Coward's *Private Lives*, and Eugene O'Neill's *Emperor Jones* reminded students and faculty members of others' pains and struggles, while university athletics provided distraction and entertainment without the shadow of the decade's grayness.

IV
The World Came Calling

IN 1939, the university basketball team won the first National Collegiate Athletic Association championship. The team, nicknamed the Tall Firs, came home in a glory that lifted spirits beyond the depression at home and on campus.

"Lauded by lines of campus undergrads, faculty, and townspeople, Oregon's favorite sons detrained in Eugene at high noon the last day of March, having defeated Ohio State at Evanston, Illinois," read one report. "Then honors, praises, and cheers flew thick and fast from Illinois to Oregon, but the basketeers remained likeably bashful."

On the track, Bill Hayward was anything but bashful. His motto for living was, as he wrote,

"Live your life so you can look any man in the face and tell him to go to hell." By 1939, his thirty-sixth year as head trainer and track coach for the university, and having coached American Olympic teams three times, Hayward was an icon of the UO, with a reputation more celebrated than even that of the newly crowned Tall Firs.

The first day of 1940 began like so many before at the university, full of the noise of work, studies, and socializing—the problems of the world in the shadowy distance. But one December morning, the university felt the world come fiercely calling.

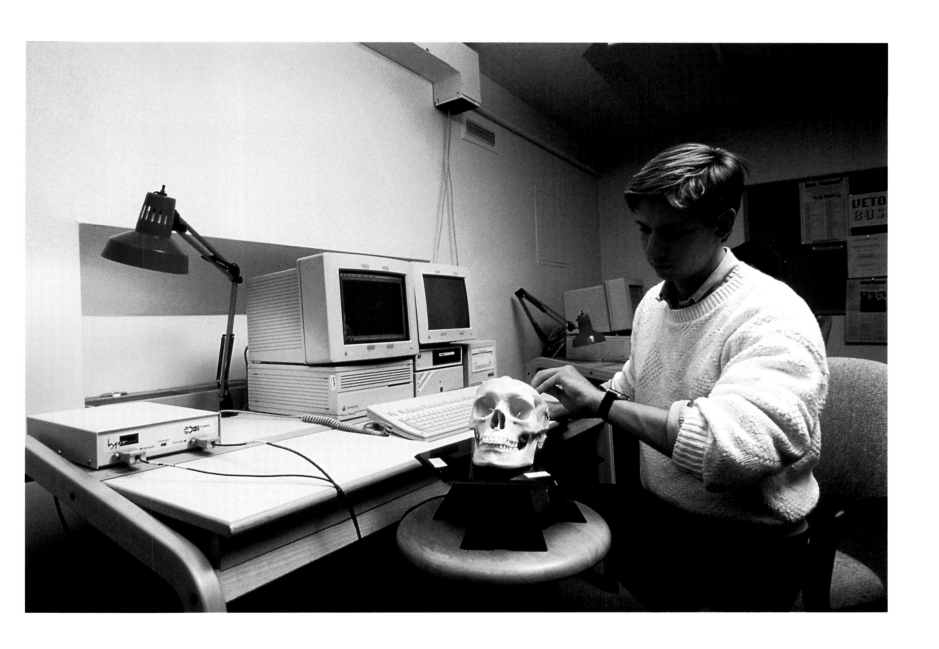

V
Good to be Back

"THE CAMPUS is blanketed with a deathly calm, a silent seriousness," a writer observed. "The College Side is no longer a gay gathering place for juke-playing collegians; instead they assemble there to listen to war news."

"Last year the word war was a strange word for present-generation university students," a 1943 *Oregana* contributor ruminated. "It was something the oldsters talked about in reminiscence; it was something you read about in history books. This year, as the draft took more and more of the boys, as food and clothing supplies became more restricted, and most importantly, as students began taking their part in the job here at home, the war became a reality on campus."

This reality was reflected in many of the university's schools and departments.

The College of Business Administration (now the Lundquist College of Business) reported that "freshmen in business administration at the University of Oregon concern themselves mainly with struggling through a maze of . . . accounting in order to better equip themselves to find a place in a world growing daily more difficult."

And the Medical School declared, "When any country goes to war, one of the first things it needs

is doctors. The University of Oregon Medical School . . . has had a year revolving around that one little word—war."

Soldiers marched on the fields south of McArthur Court, and the 1943 yearbook was dedicated to "the many students and former students who are fighting in the armed forces of the United States."

Amid the death reports from far away, news of a local loss saddened the campus. President Donald Erb died in December 1943.

As the decade progressed, students continued to leave the campus and go to war. The small Gold Star service flag commemorated those who did not come back.

Then, on an August day in 1945, in a mushroom cloud few understood, the war ended. The shadow of that cloud would hang over an entire generation of students to come—but for now, the boys were home.

Nothing described being home better than "It Is Better Now that We Are Back," written by the staff of the 1946 *Oregana*:

"It's good to be back.

"It's good to see grass, inexcusable green, impractical ivy on aged buildings, naked trees made naked not by shrapnel.

"It's good to know books . . . shelves on shelves of books . . . great numbers of them waiting for a friend. Their friend is here. . . .

"It was good to be here when we left.

"It is better now that we are back."

VI
New Challenges

As GIs returned, enrollment swelled— from 1,738 in 1943 to 6,148 in 1948.

"Students over- flowed the class-

rooms," the *Oregana* reported. "They put the administration on the hunt for more teachers and textbooks. They crowded the sidewalks and spilled over onto the grass in the rush between classes."

To accommodate the growth, Villard Hall was remodeled, additions were built onto Commerce, Condon, and Oregon halls, and plans were drawn for the Erb Memorial Union and women's dorms. A student-housing shortage was solved temporarily by the installation at Fifteenth Avenue and Agate Street of fifty-four tiny trailers—the type that families pulled behind their DeSotos on

summer outings to Crater Lake.

Life on campus again promised a sense of normalcy—although some might have ar- gued that the Roaring Twenties, the Great Depression, and two world wars had eternally changed the idea of what constituted a normal life.

The war had changed many things, yet much of the familiar remained. Social events were still reigned over by Betty Coed, the Emerald Cover Girl, Oregon's Dream Girl, the Bonds Away Girl, and Miss Hospitality. Students attended plays and social events: *The Skin of Our Teeth, Petrified Forest, School for Scandal, Glass Menagerie;* the Music Box Ball, Hoopster's Hop, Beaux Arts Ball, Heart Hop, Coed's Capers, tugs of war, Mother's Weekend.

And world-renowned musicians Arthur Rubinstein and Marian Anderson made concert appearances on the UO campus.

The decade also brought loss to many university departments. Bill Hayward died, and basketball coach Howard "Hobby" Hobson left the university for Yale. Eric Allen, longtime dean of the journalism school, died, as did Ellis F. Lawrence, university architect and dean of the School of Architecture and Allied Arts.

In basketball, the Ducks played forty-three games—twenty-two in preseason, where they went 16-6, and sixteen in the regular season, where they tallied an 11-5 record. They reached the NCAA tournament but lost in the first round.

The university football team, under coach Jim Aiken, was awarded a trip to the 1949 Cotton Bowl after being passed over for a visit to the Rose Bowl. They lost to Southern Methodist University, 21-13.

By 1950, the long-awaited Erb Memorial Union was completed and a decade full of promise was under way. World War II seemed a thing of the past. There were new challenges to be met, new opportunities to be explored.

New students attended classes in new buildings, as the University Theatre, the Music Building, and Carson Hall were completed. Villard Hall was remodeled, and a $700,000 addition was made to the library. A wing was added to the Journalism Building, now named Allen Hall, and the university established its first research center, the Institute of Molecular Biology.

VII
Growth as the Watchword

GUEST lecturers and entertainers covered the political, social, and cultural spectrum. Theodore S. Peterson, president and director of Standard Oil of California, delivered a speech entitled "Big Business Meets the Challenge of Change"; J. Robert Oppenheimer shared his views about atomic power and world peace; Linus Pauling warned about the danger of radioactive fallout; John F. Kennedy, then a Massachusetts senator, lectured on United States foreign policy. And there were others—William Faulkner, Robert Frost, Shelley Berman, Wernher von Braun, Nelson Rockefeller, Eleanor Roosevelt, Basil Rathbone, William F. Buckley, Barry Goldwater, George Wallace, Dick

Gregory. And in a controversial decision, Gus Hall, former general secretary of the Communist Party of the United States of America, was invited to speak on campus.

Students crowded the Erb Memorial Union for Friday at Four, no-date mixers, table tennis, bowling, billiards, art exhibits, and lectures.

Harry K. Newburn, selected to succeed the late Donald Erb as president of the university, resigned in 1953 to take a position with the Ford Foundation. The following year, O. Meredith Wilson came from the Ford Foundation to take over the presidency of the university.

Even with new leadership, the university did

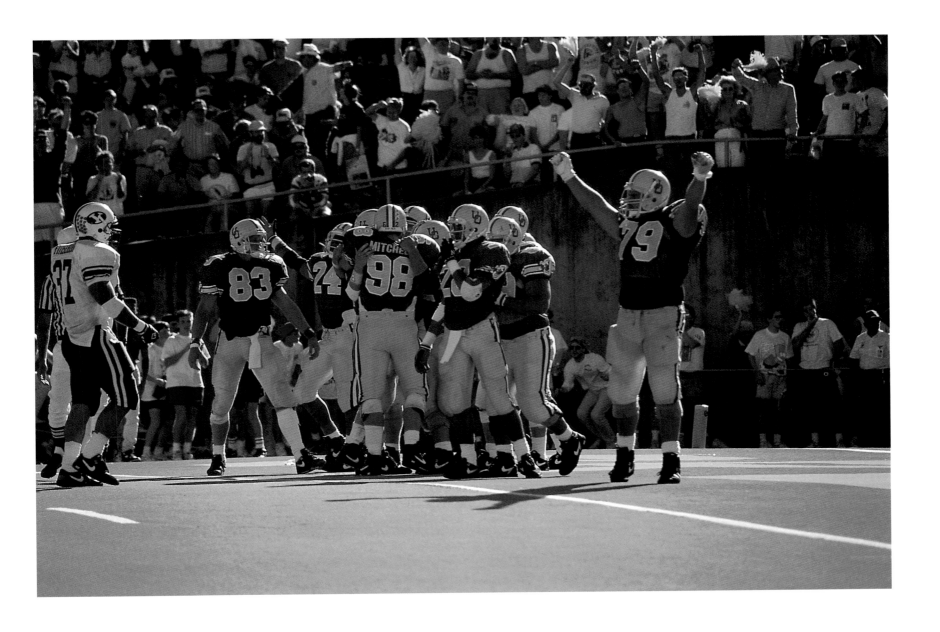

not change much in the lives of sorority and frater-nity members. The *Oregana* offered an inside look at sorority life: "Under twenty-five different roofs scattered across campus live Oregon coeds in their homes away from home . . . sharing one another's secrets and sorrows . . . circulating cashmeres and tweeds . . . thrilling to the fraternity serenades drifting up to the windows through the darkness of the night."

Meanwhile, men in the frat houses were "com-paring little black books, turning out for intramurals . . . whooping it up on weekends, not to exclude weekdays."

Men's track, coached by Bill Bowerman, show-cased Bill Dellinger, Jim Bailey, and Ken Reiser—a trio who gained an international reputation. The team finished fourth in the NCAA championship meet. Bailey and Dellinger were chosen to compete in the Olympics. Bailey broke the four-minute-mile barrier, the first person to do so on American soil.

The 1957 football team made it to the Rose Bowl. And even though they lost to Ohio State University, 10-7, coach Len Casanova called the players "the most amazing team I ever coached."

And Casanova, who coached from 1951 to 1966, was an amazing coach. The winningest coach in the school's history, he led his teams to three postseason bowl appearances and began his final season in 1966 as the fourteenth-winningest head coach in the country. His players included Bob Berry, Jack Crabtree, Jack Patera, Mel Renfro, John Robinson, Jim Shanley, George Shaw, Willie West, and Dave Wilcox.

As the decade came to an end, the 1957 *Oregana* staff captured the essence of 1950s campus life: "Coffee and concentration and diversion in the Side . . . registration cards and blue books and drop cards . . . seven o'clock eggs and eight o'clock fog and nine o'clock lab . . . ink-stained fingers and broken pencils."

Goals for the future of the university were set by the administration, with growth as the watchword. But some students opposed increasing the university enrollment and expanding the facilities.

One student recalled, "The teacher said that attendance was not mandatory, that he didn't even care if we came. This was a shock to me. We went into class, sat down, and our names were read. Like numbers. That was the end of personal contact. It seemed so cold."

Others expressed a more positive, if not serious, view of campus life. "Spring is not the season for studying," wrote another student. "We'd rather pursue each other than academic excellence."

In the *Oregana*, student writer Ted Mahar added another perspective:

"To put fall term 1961 in its proper historical perspective, John F. Kennedy's 'New Frontier' administration was not yet one year old. As students came to the university, some for the first time, some for the last, thousands of East German refugees were attempting to flee to West Berlin.

"Not quite a month before fall term began, President Kennedy had trebled the draft. There would, he said, be hardships: families would be disrupted, careers would be postponed, studies would be interrupted. The tension was audible in those students most likely to be affected. . . .

". . . and so fall term 1961 ground down to finals week while the eternal rain drizzled across the campus. Time now exacted its price for hours wasted. The mortar drying between the bricks of the Berlin Wall caused less worry than final exams. Through momentarily fatigued eyes students look forward to the dead of winter, a new term, a new year."

VIII
On a Clear Morning

ON COLUMBUS Day 1963, Typhoon Frieda, better known as the Columbus Day Storm, toppled trees, crushed cars, and blew a swath of destruction across the state. Dozens of trees on campus, many from the first days of the university, were destroyed.

The foundation of patriotism and civic loyalty was also uprooted as Vietnam and civil rights became the focal points of frustration at a university known for both its conservative heritage and its intellectual openness. Students had marched for peace at the University of Oregon in the 1930s, but this was different.

The feelings ran deeper and the actions became more passionately demonstrated—and more violently released.

An all-night anti-Vietnam War demonstration was organized, and in front of the microphones were Wayne Morse, Ernest Greuning, and Charles Porter.

Allen Ginsberg's *Howl* was read at the Erb Memorial Union's Free Speech Platform, the ROTC building was burned, windows were broken continually, and Prince Lucien Campbell and Johnson halls were bombed.

The 1968 *Oregana* publicly examined its

editorial stance: "Shall we tell it like it really is? Or should we go along creating a storybook campus and fluffy yearbook essays that say nothing?"

Finally, as the 1960s came to an end, the big snow of 1969 did what demonstrations had been unable to do—close the campus and keep the 15,200 students out of classes for one day.

"The movements [of the 1960s]," said Robert Clark, university president from 1969 to 1975, "left a legacy, a new consciousness on the part of students, an unrelenting concern for justice, for the rights of minorities, for the rights of women, for protection of the environment, and for the development of a curriculum to reflect the cultural diversity in our society."

For more than 100 years, each generation has contributed to the legacy that is the University of Oregon—a legacy supported by the same spirit of generosity and vision that enabled the doors of Deady Hall to open in 1876 and built the Museum of Art in 1930 and the four-building science complex in 1990.

A number of recent private contributions have enabled the University of Oregon to expand and add state-of-the-art instructional, research, and athletic facilities. These include the Bowerman Family Building, the Leonard B. Casanova Athletic Center, the Earle A. Chiles Business Center, and the Knight Library. Major gifts of endowment are enhancing the quality of university programs

ranging from science to music to business. Of special significance are the Alec and Kay Keith Fund for Biology, Physics, and Chemistry and an endowment from Charles H. Lundquist for the Lundquist College of Business.

Today the University of Oregon is a campus that builds pride in the standing of its faculty, a campus whose schools and departments are ranked among the best in the nation.

It is a university with nine faculty members who belong to the National Academy of Sciences, seven to the American Academy of Arts and Sciences, and eleven faculty members who are named Presidential Young Investigators by the National Science Foundation.

Students come to today's campus for what they have always sought—the joy of life-long friendships, the challenge of the classroom, and the sound of spring on the walk between Deady and Friendly halls.

They come for all the reasons and with all the feelings and thoughts of anyone who struggles across a landscape of unexplored ideas, time, and dreams.

And looking up from the valley on a clear morning, they see majestic snowy peaks shouldering through that ragged gap in the Cascades, north-facing hills eroded by the ages, a western mountain range that turns to shadows at sunset— a landscape of promise and hope.

LIST OF PHOTOGRAPHS